# Explore the Sights of

# BERLIN

# DIVIDED–UNITED
# Geteilt–Vereint

## Cultural Guide & Coloring Book

CULTURE TO COLOR

For the artist in you - coloring adventures around the globe. No suitcase necessary!

## Bibi LeBlanc

# A BRIEF HISTORY

*"Ich bin ein Berliner!" – "I am a Berliner"*

Thank you for choosing this Berlin coloring book! With *Berlin Divided – Berlin United* I would like to show you the beautiful sights of Berlin as well as tell you a story about its not-so-distant past: Berlin during the Cold War and what it was like to live in a city divided by a wall. I grew up in West Berlin. This is my personal story.

Let me take you back a few years ...

World War II ended in 1945. Germany was divided into four zones of occupation by the winning allied forces, the U.S., France, England and the Soviet Union.

The capital, Berlin, was in the Soviet zone and also divided: West Berlin (U.S., English and French sectors) and East Berlin (Soviet sector). Construction of the Berlin Wall started the night of August 13, 1961, because at that point thousands of people were leaving the Soviet sector every day to escape communist oppression. The next morning, many Berlin residents found themselves cut off from work, school, family and friends.

In his famous speech in West Berlin on June 26th, 1963, John F. Kennedy declared to the world: "I am a Berliner." His message was aimed as much at Berliners and West Germans as at the East German and Soviet governments. It was a clear statement of U.S. policy in the wake of the construction of the Berlin Wall, and a morale boost for West Berliners fearing communist occupation at any moment.

I was born in the American Sector in West Berlin three months after that speech. Two years after the Berlin Wall was built. I grew up with it. The wall running through the middle of my hometown became part of my everyday reality.

Across the street were houses we could not visit because the wall was in between. We could not just drive out of the city to the countryside because we were enclosed by a wall which was guarded by sharpshooters in watchtowers, electric fences and guard dogs patrolling a strip of minefields called the *death strip*.

My dad's brother and his family lived in East Berlin. We could visit them. They could never visit us. We had to apply for a *Passierschein*, a passage pass, a lengthy process, that would allow us to cross at one of the few checkpoints.

As a child, crossing into East Berlin was quite scary. There was an atmosphere of harassment and intimidation, and often waiting times of several hours. The *Vopos*, short for *Volkspolizei* or *The People's Police*, made us get out of the car so that they could search it. They would lift up the back seat. They would stick a long flexible rod into the gas tank. They would check the underside of our car with a mirror on little wheels to see if we were smuggling anything.

We were only allowed to bring certain things like clothes and food. Any printed material, for example, was considered illegal "capitalist propaganda." Knowing my dad often smuggled things made the experience of crossing the border into East Berlin even scarier.

We knew the apartment my aunt and uncle and cousins lived in was bugged. We suspected the neighbors were *IMs* (Informelle Mitarbeiter - informal collaborators) for the Stasi, the East-German Ministry for State Security.

The Stasi has been described as one of the most effective and repressive intelligence and secret police agencies ever to have existed. One of its main tasks was to spy on the population mainly through a vast network of citizens-turned-informants. For any citizen to tell a joke about the government or the general secretary, the government leader, would be enough grounds for the Stasi to arrest, incarcerate and interrogate that citizen, and force him or her to "work" with them as an informal collaborator.

My parents would go for long walks by the river with my aunt and uncle because they couldn't talk freely in the apartment. Even we children had to be careful what we talked about.

There is a lot more I could tell you about growing up in West Berlin, but that would exceed the scope of this introduction. Let me fast-forward a few years ...

In 1989, I was a Lufthansa flight attendant based in Frankfurt, West Germany. One November day I returned from a trip to Africa when my mom called and said: "The wall just fell." At first, I couldn't comprehend what she was saying. I did not think I would *ever* see that wall coming down. It was just that much a part of my reality!

My roommates and I jumped into the car and started driving toward Berlin. On the Autobahn we saw *Trabis*, the East German cars, which we had never seen there before.

Remember, we had to drive through East Germany to get to Berlin. When we reached the first border-crossing checkpoint in Helmstedt around 11 p.m. on this dark, cold night, there were cars parked on both sides of the Autobahn, which on any normal day was illegal.

The atmosphere was full of laughter and rejoicing as Trabis from East Germany, loaded to the max with people, were coming through the checkpoint, being welcomed by West Germans with thermos bottles of tea and hot chocolate. We were laughing, crying tears of joy and hugging as we all became part of history in the making.

Later that night we arrived in Berlin, connected with family and headed straight to the Brandenburg Gate. It had been the symbol of Berlin and German division for the past 28 years. No man's land. Neither West Berliners nor East Berliners could walk through it. On this night, we did!

On November 9th each year, the world celebrates the anniversary of the fall of the Berlin Wall.

And since that day in 1989, whenever I face challenges and circumstances that seem impossible to change, I remind myself of those days and the fall of the Berlin Wall - of my reality crumbling, the course of world history changing right before my eyes. And I know anything is possible!

This is my personal story. Even as a child, I always considered myself the fortunate one, having grown up in West Berlin, not East Berlin. Being able to speak my mind, without the constant fear of being spied on by friends, neighbors or co-workers, and my ability to travel the world were freedoms the people of East Berlin longed for under communist rule.

I would like to encourage you to go out and talk to people who experienced the reality of life in divided Berlin. You'll be amazed, intrigued, shocked, and touched by the stories people have to share.

In the meantime, I'd like to leave you with this:

*Go visit your family – because you can.*
*Go travel the world – because you can.*
*Go live your dreams – because you can!*

*If you'd like to learn more about what life in divided Berlin was like, check out the resource section in the back of this book. There are some interesting movies, TV series and, of course, books that do an excellent job describing life in Berlin during the Cold War.*

## Welcome to Berlin

From cultural exhibitions to pop concerts and street festivals, Berlin is exciting 365 days of the year, and offers something for every taste every day of every month, all year long.

In this coloring book, on the occasion of the 30th anniversary of the fall of the Berlin Wall, I would like to take you on a journey through its not-so-distant history — a journey through the once divided and now united Berlin.
*Welcome to my hometown Berlin*!

## Willkommen in Berlin

Von Kultur über Ausstellungen bis hin zu Popkonzerten und Straßenfesten ist Berlin an 365 Tagen im Jahr aufregend. Es bietet rund ums Jahr etwas für jeden Geschmack.

In diesem Malbuch möchte ich Sie, aus Anlass des 30. Jahrestages des Mauerfalls, auf eine Reise in die nicht so ferne Geschichte Berlins mitnehmen - eine Reise durch das einst geteilte und nun wieder vereinte Berlin.
*Willkommen in meiner Heimatstadt Berlin*!

WELCOME TO BERLIN

# Germany Divided

At the Potsdam Conference in 1945, the Allies divided defeated Germany into American,
British, French and Soviet zones of occupation. The capital Berlin, though in the Soviet
zone, was also divided. Even though it was supposed to be a temporary division,
two German countries were founded in the late 1940s, the Federal Republic
of Germany (FRG) and the German Democratic Republic (GDR).
After the peaceful revolution in the GDR and the fall of the Berlin Wall in 1989,
reunification of both parts of the country followed in 1990.

# Geteiltes Deutschland

Auf der Potsdamer Konferenz 1945 teilten die Alliierten das besiegte Deutschland in
amerikanische, britische, französische und sowjetische Besatzungszonen auf.  Die
Hauptstadt Berlin, in der Sowjetzone gelegen, wurde ebenfalls geteilt. Obwohl es sich
um eine vorübergehende Teilung handeln sollte, wurden Ende der 40er Jahre zwei
deutsche Länder gegründet, die Bundesrepublik Deutschland (BRD) und die
Deutsche Demokratische Republik (DDR). Nach der friedlichen Revolution in der DDR
und dem Mauerfall 1989 folgte 1990 die Wiedervereinigung beider Landesteile.

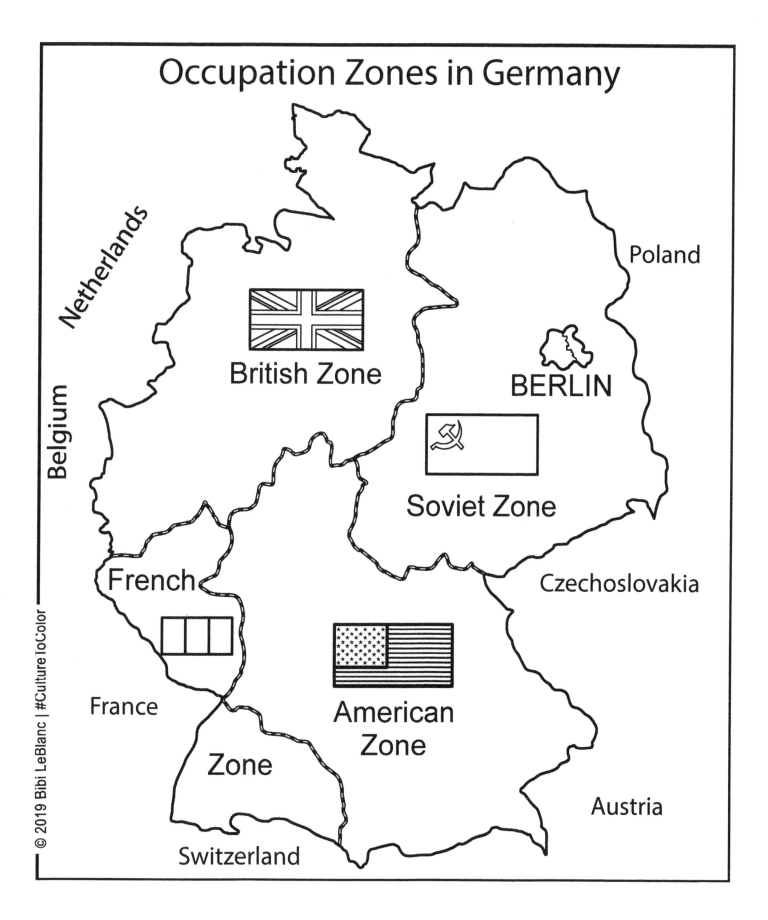

# Occupation Zones in Germany

Netherlands

Belgium

Poland

British Zone

BERLIN

Soviet Zone

France

French

Czechoslovakia

American Zone

Zone

Austria

Switzerland

© 2019 Bibi LeBlanc | #CultureToColor

# GETEILTES DEUTSCHLAND
# GERMANY DIVIDED

## Kaiser Wilhelm Gedächtniskirche – Memorial Church
## Kurfürstendamm

The *Gedächtniskirche* is one of Berlins striking landmarks. The ruin of the church
on Kurfürstendamm is now a peace memorial.
One of the most famous streets in the world, *Kurfürstendamm* or *Ku'damm*, was built
in the 16th century as a bridle path. Later it became a boulevard with theaters, cafés
and shops, based on the French model. Stroll along Ku'damm where old and new
architecture meet almost seamlessly, peruse elegant shop windows or enjoy
a cappuccino in one of the plentiful street cafés.


## Kaiser Wilhelm Gedächtniskirche am Kurfürstendamm

Die *Gedächtniskirche* ist eines der bekanntesten Wahrzeichen Berlins. Die Ruine
der Kirche am *Kurfürstendamm* wurde in ein Mahnmal für Frieden
und Versöhnung umgewandelt.
Eine der berühmtesten Straßen der Welt - der *Kurfürstendamm*, auch *Ku'damm*
genannt - wurde im 16. Jahrhundert als Reitweg gebaut. Später wurde er nach
französischem Vorbild zu einer Prachtstraße mit Theatern, Cafés und exklusiven
Geschäften. Machen Sie einen Schaufensterbummel entlang des Ku'damms, wo alte
und neue Architektur fast nahtlos zusammentreffen ... oder geniessen Sie einen
Cappuccino in einem der zahlreichen Straßen-Cafés.

Kurfürstendamm

KAISER WILHELM GEDÄCHTNISKIRCHE
MEMORIAL CHURCH — KURFÜRSTENDAMM

## Siegessäule – Victory Column

The *Siegessäule* with Victoria, Goddess of Victory, was built by Friedrich Drake and has reinvented itself through the ages — from a symbol of Prussian military victory in the 19th century to a favorite tourist spot today. In the center of a roundabout, the column is accessible through four tunnels. It's well worth climbing the 285-step spiral staircase to see the spectacular view from the observation deck. — In 2008, U.S. presidential candidate Barack Obama chose the Siegessäule for his speech to 200,000 Berliners.

## Siegessäule

Die *Siegessäule* im Tiergarten mit Victoria, der Göttin des Sieges, wurde von Friedrich Drake erbaut und hat sich im Laufe der Jahrhunderte neu erfunden - vom Symbol des Sieges der preußischen Streitkräfte im 19. Jahrhundert bis zum beliebten Touristenort. Die von einem Kreisverkehr umgebene Säule ist durch vier Tunnel zugänglich. Das Besteigen der 285-stufigen Wendeltreppe ist den spektakulären Blick von der Aussichtsplattform wert. — 2008 wählte US-Präsidentschaftskandidat Barack Obama die Siegessäule für seine Rede vor 200.000 Berlinern.

SIEGESSÄULE — VICTORY COLUMN

# Berlin Wall

The *Berlin Wall* was a 12-foot-tall concrete barrier that physically and ideologically divided Berlin from 1961 to 1989. Construction began the night of August 13, 1961, to stop East Berliners from fleeing communist oppression. The next morning many Berlin residents found themselves cut off from work, school, family and friends. The wall was guarded by sharpshooters in watchtowers, electric fences and guard dogs patrolling a strip of mine fields called the "death strip."

# Berliner Mauer

Die *Berliner Mauer* war eine 3,60 m hohe Betonbarriere, die Ost- und West-Berlin von 1961 bis 1989 physisch und ideologisch trennte. Die Bauarbeiten begannen in der Nacht des 13. August 1961, um die täglich tausenden Ost-Berliner von der Flucht aus der Sowjetzone abzuhalten. Am nächsten Morgen waren viele Berliner plötzlich von ihrem Arbeitsplatz, der Schule, Familie und Freunden abgeschnitten. Die Mauer wurde von Scharfschützen in Wachtürmen bewacht, elektrischen Zäunen und ausgebildeten Hunden, die den „Todesstreifen" patroullierten.

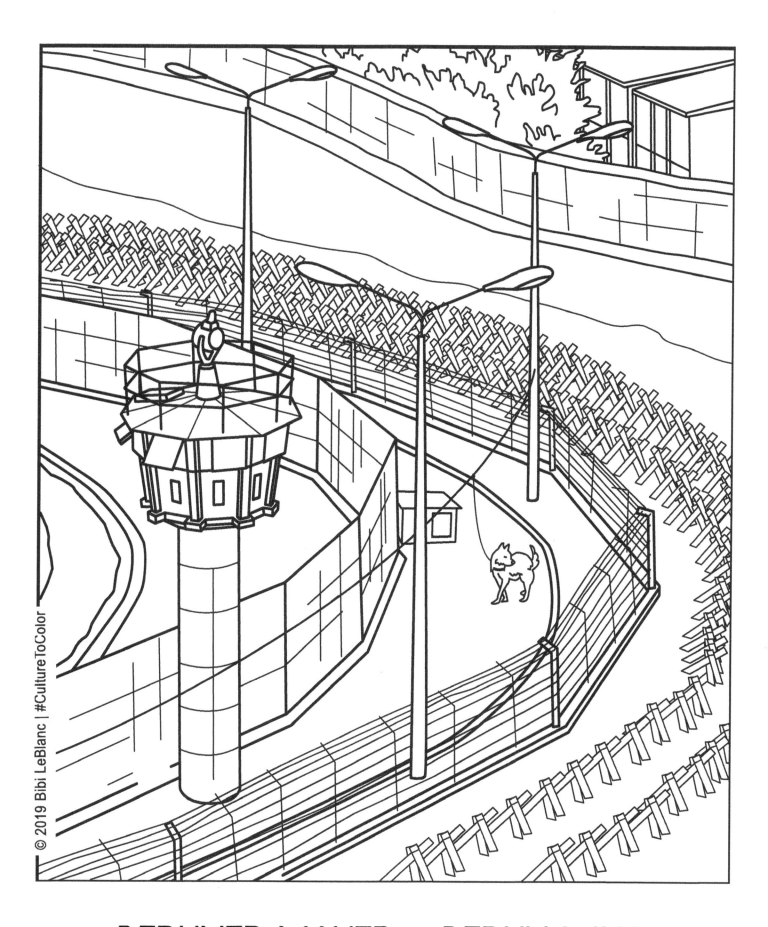

BERLINER MAUER — BERLIN WALL

## Alexanderplatz, Urania World Clock & TV Tower

*Alexanderplatz*, or *Alex*, is one of Berlin's liveliest places.
The *Urania World Clock*, a popular meeting spot, shows the time in 148 cities.
The *TV Tower*, the tallest structure in Germany (1,200 feet), was built to be both a symbol of the city and socialist power. A revolving sphere restaurant at 679 feet and observation deck and bar at 665 feet offer spectacular views of this bustling city.
In 1989, the peaceful demonstrations against the East German government culminated here at Alexanderplatz.

## Alexanderplatz, Urania Weltzeituhr & Fernsehturm

Der *Alexanderplatz*, von den Einheimischen *Alex* genannt, ist einer der belebtesten Orte Berlins. Die *Urania-Weltzeituhr* zeigt die Uhrzeit von 148 Städten der Welt an und ist ein beliebter Treffpunkt. Der *Fernsehturm*, Deutschlands höchstes Gebäude (368 m), wurde sowohl als Symbol der Stadt als auch sozialistischer Macht gebaut. Die Aussichtsetage mit Bar auf 203 m und das Drehrestaurant auf 207 m bieten einen spektakulären Blick auf Berlin. 1989 konzentrierten sich die friedlichen Demonstrationen gegen die DDR-Regierung hier am Alexanderplatz.

# ALEXANDERPLATZ
# URANIA WORLD CLOCK AND TV TOWER

## Viewing Platform

The Berlin Wall (1961 – 1989) was one of the most powerful and iconic symbols of the Cold War. *Viewing platforms* were built on the west side of the wall. West Berliners and visitors could climb up to get a glimpse of the world behind the Iron Curtain and the barren "death strip" that geographically and politically separated East Berlin from West Berlin.

## Aussichtsplattform

Die Berliner Mauer war eines der mächtigsten und bekanntesten Symbole des Kalten Krieges. Auf der Westseite der Mauer wurden *Aussichtsplattformen* errichtet. West-Berliner und Touristen konnten von hier einen Blick hinter den Eisernen Vorhang auf den kargen „Todesstreifen" werfen, der Ost- und West-Berlin physisch und politisch trennte.

AUSSICHTSPLATTFORM
VIEWING PLATFORM

# John F. Kennedy in West Berlin

U.S. President *John F. Kennedy* (1917 – 1963) has been a legend in the German capital since his speech on June 26, 1963. Speaking from a platform at Rathaus Schöneberg to an audience of 450,000, Kennedy said, "Two thousand years ago, the proudest boast was *'civis romanus sum'* (I am a Roman citizen). Today, in a world of freedom, the proudest boast is *'Ich bin ein Berliner!'"* JFK pledging the full might of the U.S. to defend West Berlin was a great morale boost for West Berliners fearing Soviet occupation.

# John F. Kennedy in West Berlin

U.S. President *John F. Kennedy* (1917 – 1963) ist seit seiner Rede am 26. Juni 1963 eine Legende in der deutschen Hauptstadt. Am Rathaus Schöneberg sagte Kennedy vor 450.000 Zuschauern: „Vor zweitausend Jahren war das stolzeste Prahlen ‚civis romanus sum' (Ich bin römischer Staatsbürger). Heute, in der Welt der Freiheit, ist es ‚*Ich bin ein Berliner*!'" Es war ein großer Moralschub für West-Berliner, die sich vor einer sowjetischen Besetzung fürchteten.

All free men, wherever they may live,
are citizens of Berlin.
And therefore, as a free man,
I take pride in the words

*'Ich bin ein Berliner!'*
*(I am a Berliner)*

- John F. Kennedy -

JOHN F. KENNEDY IN WEST BERLIN

## Staatsoper – Berlin State Opera - Unter den Linden

The *Staatsoper*, commonly referred to as Lindenoper, is the home of the Berlin State Opera Company. Despite the construction of the Berlin Wall in 1961 and the restrictions that followed, the Staatsoper managed to retain its international reputation. Today, under the musical direction of Daniel Barenboim, the Lindenoper ranks among the world's leading opera houses.

## Staatsoper

Die *Staatsoper*, im Volksmund Lindenoper genannt, ist die Heimat der Berliner Staatsoper. Trotz des Baus der Berliner Mauer im Jahr 1961 und den sich daraus ergebenden Einschränkungen gelang es der Staatsoper, ihren internationalen Ruf zu bewahren. Heute zählt die Lindenoper unter der musikalischen Leitung von Daniel Barenboim zu den weltweit führenden Opernhäusern.

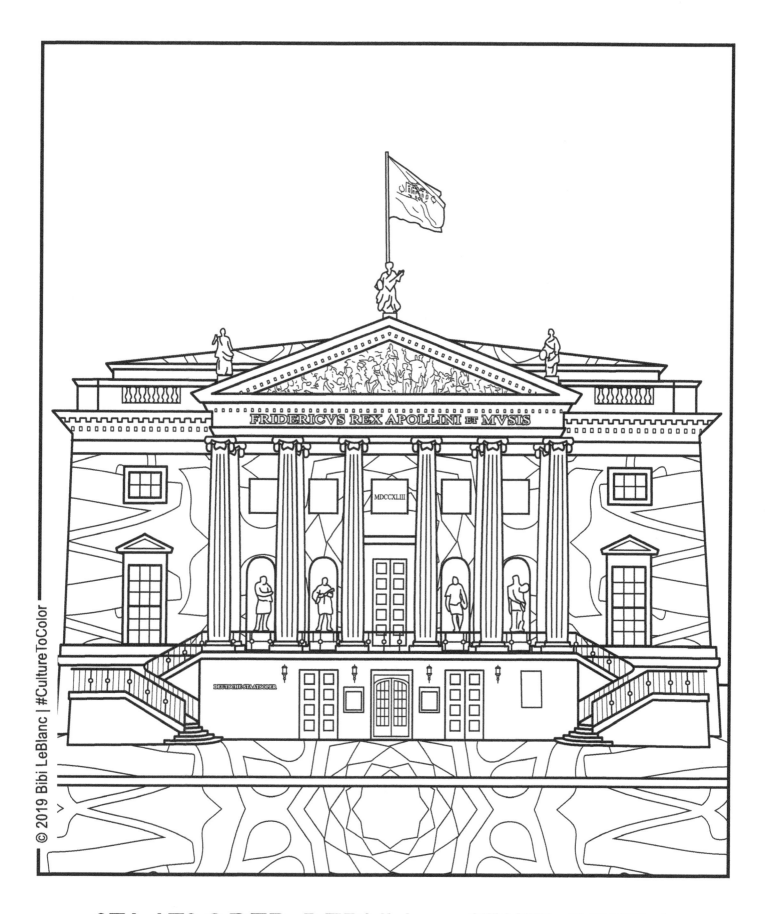

FRIDERICVS REX APOLLINI ET MVSIS

MDCCXLIII

DEUTSCHE STAATSOPER

# STAATSOPER BERLIN — STATE OPERA
# UNTER DEN LINDEN

## Checkpoint Charlie & Wall Museum - Haus am Checkpoint Charlie

*Checkpoint Charlie* was the best-known crossing point between East and West Berlin for members of the armed forces during the Cold War. It is the setting for many spy novels and movies. Visit the nearby *Wall Museum - Haus am Checkpoint Charlie* to relive those days and learn about successful escapes and the courage of people whose desire for freedom was greater than their fear.

## Checkpoint Charlie & Mauermuseum - Haus am Checkpoint Charlie

*Checkpoint Charlie* war während des Kalten Krieges der bekannteste Grenzübergang zwischen Ost- und West-Berlin für Angehörige der Streitkräfte. Er ist der Schauplatz vieler Spionageromane und Filme. Besuchen Sie das nahe gelegene *Mauer Museum - Haus am Checkpoint Charlie*, um diese Tage noch einmal zu erleben und mehr über erfolgreiche Fluchten zu erfahren und den Mut von Menschen, deren Wunsch nach Freiheit größer war als ihre Angst.

CHECKPOINT CHARLIE AND WALL MUSEUM
HAUS AM CHECKPOINT CHARLIE

## Hotel Adlon Kempinski

Originally built by Lorenz Adlon in 1907 as Berlin's most luxurious hotel, *Hotel Adlon Kempinski* has hosted people from across the globe, including royalty and movie stars. It is located on famous Unter den Linden street with a view of the Brandenburg Gate at Pariser Platz. Although it was largely destroyed in 1945, the Adlon has been rebuilt with a design inspired by the original. The Hotel Adlon continues to attract and fascinate guests from around the world.

## Hotel Adlon Kempinski

Das ursprünglich 1907 von Lorenz Adlon als Berlins luxuriösestes Hotel erbaute *Hotel Adlon Kempinski* war Gastgeber für Reisende aus aller Welt, einschliesslich Königen und Filmstars. Es befindet sich Unter den Linden mit Blick auf das Brandenburger Tor am Pariser Platz. Nachdem es 1945 größtenteils zerstört wurde, ist das heutige Hotel Adlon Kempinski ein neues - vom Originaldesign inspiriertes - Gebäude, und zieht Gäste aus aller Welt an.

HOTEL ADLON KEMPINSKI

# Funkturm Berlin

The *Funkturm Berlin* (radio tower) is a striking symbol of Berlin. The 482 foot tall
tower was built between 1924 - 1926 as a large steel framework structure,
similar to the Eiffel Tower in Paris. Nicknamed *Langer Lulatsch* (lanky lad),
the Funkturm is no longer used for broadcasting purposes. Visitors can enjoy
the spectacular view of the city from the restaurant at 180 feet or
the observation deck at 410 feet.

# Berliner Funkturm

Der *Berliner Funkturm* ist markantes Wahrzeichen Berlins. Der Turm mit einer Höhe
von 147 m, wurde zwischen 1924 – 1926 als Stahlkonstruktion gebaut, dem
Eiffelturm in Paris ähnlich. Der Funkturm, von Berlinern auch liebevoll „Langer
Lulatsch" genannt, wird inzwischen nicht mehr für Rundfunkzwecke verwendet.
Besucher können einen spektakulären Blick über die Stadt vom Restaurant in
55 m Höhe oder der Aussichtsplattform in 126 m geniessen.

MESSE BERLIN

# FUNKTURM BERLIN

## Elephant Gate – Zoo & Tierpark

Enter the *Zoologischer Garten* through the *Elephant Gate* for a trip around the world to meet exotic creatures. Berlin's animals have two homes in the urban jungle: *Zoo Berlin*, home to the world's largest variety of species, and *Tierpark Berlin*, Europe's largest zoo. Founded in 1955, *Tierpark* was originally established as counterpart to the West Berlin Zoo, then out of reach for residents of East Berlin. Since German reunification, both zoos have complemented each other.

## Elefantentor am Zoologischen Garten & Tierpark

Treten sie durch das *Elefantentor* in den *Zoologischen Garten* und bereisen Sie die Welt exotischer Geschöpfe. Berlins Tiere haben im Großstadtdschungel zwei Heimatorte: den Zoo Berlin, der die größte Artenvielfalt der Welt beheimatet, und den *Tierpark Berlin*, Europas größtem Zoo. Der Tierpark wurde 1955 als Gegenstück zum Zoo Berlin gegründet, der sich damals in West-Berlin befand und für die Bewohner Ost-Berlins unzugänglich war. Seit der deutschen Wiedervereinigung ergänzen sich die beiden Zoologischen Gärten.

ELEFANTENTOR — ELEPHANT GATE — ZOO

# Wall Peckers

The demolition of the Berlin Wall began soon after the border opened in 1989. Knocking and hammering, so-called *wall peckers* broke off pieces as souvenirs and removed the façade of the Berlin Wall piece by piece. Not even the loudspeaker announcements of the West Berlin police could stop them from gathering souvenirs of freedom. Pieces of the wall are sold all over the world. In June 1990, the government began the systematic dismantling of the wall and preserved some of the first sections as historical monuments.

# Mauerspechte

Bald nach der Öffnung der Grenze begann der Abriss der Mauer. Sogenannte *Mauerspechte* entfernten Stück für Stück die Fassade der Berliner Mauer. Nicht einmal die Lautsprecheransagen der West-Berliner Polizei konnten sie abhalten, diese Souvenirs der Freiheit zu sammeln. Heute werden immer noch auf der ganzen Welt Mauerstücke verkauft. Im Juni 1990 begann die Regierung den systematischen Abbau der Grenzanlagen.
Die ersten Segmente der Mauer wurden unter Denkmalschutz gestellt.

MAUERSPECHTE — WALL PECKERS

# Mikhail Gorbachev

*Mikhail Sergeyevich Gorbachev* (1931 -  ), a Soviet politician, was the initiator of a series of events that transformed the political fabric of Europe and marked the beginning of the end of the Cold War. As general secretary of the Central Committee of the Communist Party of the Soviet Union (1985 – 1991), he set new directions for Soviet politics with glasnost (openness) and perestroika (reconstruction). In disarmament negotiations with the United States, he initiated the end of the Cold War.
In 1990, he received the Nobel Peace Prize.


# Michail Gorbatschow

*Michail Sergejewitsch Gorbatschow* (1931 - ), ein sowjetischer Politiker, war der Initiator einer Reihe von Ereignissen, die das politische Gefüge Europas veränderten und den Beginn des Endes des Kalten Krieges markierten. Als Generalsekretär des Zentralkomitees der Kommunistischen Partei der Sowjetunion (1985 – 1991) setzte er mit Glasnost (Offenheit) und Perestroika (Wiederaufbau) neue Akzente in der Sowjetpolitik. In Abrüstungsverhandlungen mit den USA leitete er das Ende des Kalten Krieges ein. 1990 erhielt er den Friedensnobelpreis.

"History teaches us, however, that when the times are ripe for change and the government refuses or is unable to change, either society starts to decay or a revolution begins."

- Mikhail Gorbachev, On My Country and the World

MIKHAIL GORBACHEV

## Berlin Divided

After the end of World War II in 1945, defeated Germany was divided into Soviet, American, British and French zones of occupation. Berlin, though geographically part of the Soviet zone, was also split with the Soviets taking the eastern part of the city. By 1961, thousands of East Germans, including many skilled laborers, professionals and intellectuals, were leaving the Soviet sector every day to escape communist oppression. Shortly after midnight on August 13th, 1961, East German soldiers began laying down barbed wire and bricks as a barrier between communist-controlled East Berlin and the democratic western sectors, and thus began the construction of the Berlin Wall.

## Geteiltes Berlin

Nach dem Zweiten Weltkrieg wurde das besiegte Deutschland 1945 in sowjetische, amerikanische, britische und französische Besatzungszonen aufgeteilt. Obwohl Berlin geografisch in der Sowjetzone lag, wurde es ebenfalls geteilt, wobei die Sowjets den östlichen Teil der Stadt einnahmen. Bis 1961 verließen Ostdeutsche täglich zu Tausenden den sowjetischen Sektor, darunter viele Fachkräfte und Intellektuelle. Um das zu verhindern, begannen ostdeutsche Soldaten kurz nach Mitternacht des 13. August 1961 Stacheldraht und Ziegelsteine als Barriere zwischen dem kommunistisch kontrollierten Ost-Berlin und dem demokratischen Westen zu bauen. Damit begann der Bau der Berliner Mauer.

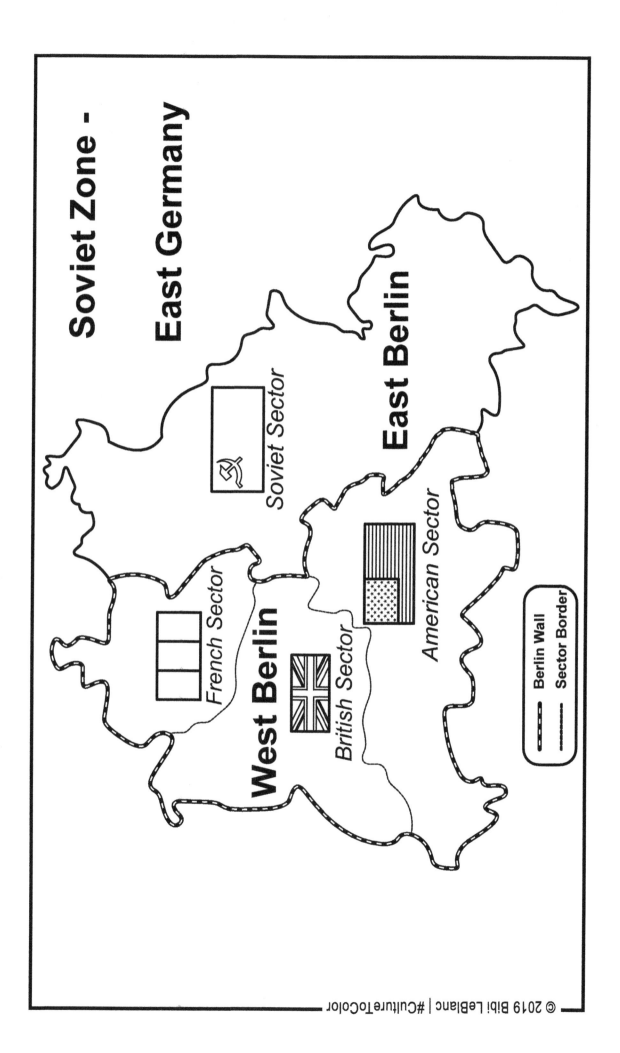

GETEILTES BERLIN — BERLIN DIVIDED

## Berlin Blockade & Airlift Candy Bombers

In a bid to force the Western Allies from Berlin in June 1948, the Soviets closed all access to the city "for repairs." The *Blockade of Berlin* led to supply shortages for the 2.2 million people living there. The only access was via three air corridors, and the Western Allies started an *airlift*. Every *three minutes*, an aircraft landed at Berlin airports for almost one year. Col. Gail Halvorsen became known for rocking his wings and dropping candy parachutes to the children during approach. "Candy bombers" delivered 326,406 tons of supplies in 278,228 flights. After 322 days, the Berlin Blockade was finally lifted.

## Berlin Blockade & Luftbrücke

Im Versuch, die westlichen Verbündeten aus Berlin zu vertreiben, sperrten im Juni 1948 die Sowjets alle Zugänge nach Berlin „für Reparaturen". Die *Blockade Berlins* führte zu Versorgungsengpässen für die 2,2 Millionen Menschen. Der einzige Zugang waren drei Luftkorridore, und die West-Alliierten begannen eine *Luftbrücke*. Fast ein Jahr landete alle drei Minuten ein Flugzeug auf den Berliner Flughäfen. Oberst Gail Halvorsen wurde dafür bekannt, dass er während des Anflugs mit den Flügeln wackelte und Süßigkeiten an Taschentuch-Fallschirmen für die Kinder abwarf. Die „Rosinenbomber" lieferten auf 278.228 Flügen 326.406 Tonnen Vorräte. Nach 322 Tagen wurde die Berliner Blockade endlich aufgehoben.

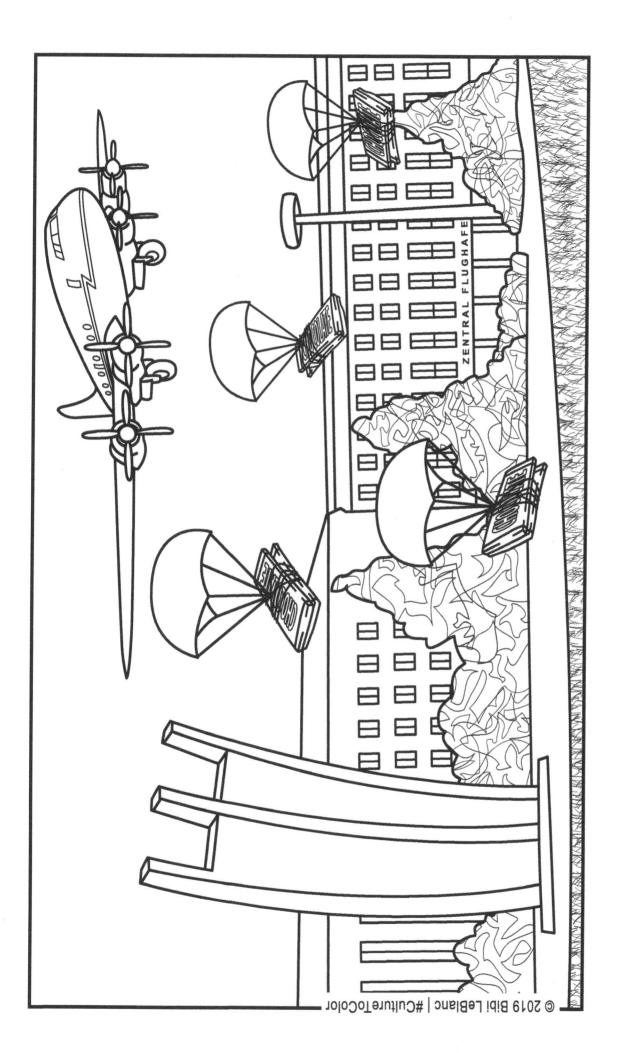

BERLIN BLOCKADE AND AIRLIFT CANDY BOMBERS

# Heilandskirche Sacrow – Church of the Redeemer

The *Heilandskirche*, a small church with a campanile (separate bell tower) on a lakeside cove, resembles a ship at harbor. During the Cold War the border between East and West Berlin ran right through it. After the Christmas service in 1961, East German border guards vandalized the church and later sealed it off to prevent escape attempts. Isolated in no man's land, the church was left to decay. On Christmas Eve 1989, weeks after the Berlin Wall fell, the congregation celebrated a Christmas service once again in the still-ruined church.

Today, after extensive restoration, church services, concerts and weddings are held at this romantic jewel of a church.

# Heilandskirche Sacrow

Die *Heilandskirche*, eine kleine Kirche mit Kampanile (separater Glockenturm), sieht aus wie ein Schiff im Hafen. Während des Kalten Krieges verlief die Grenze zu West-Berlin mitten durch die Kirche. Nach einem Weihnachtsgottesdienst im Jahr 1961 wurde sie von ostdeutschen Grenzpolizisten verwüstet und später abgeriegelt, um Fluchtversuche zu verhindern. Die im Niemandsland gefangene Kirche war dem Verfall überlassen. Am Heiligabend 1989, kurz nach dem Fall des Eisernen Vorhangs, feierte die Gemeinde in der immer noch zerstörten Kirche erneut einen Weihnachtsgottesdienst. Nach umfangreichen Renovierungen finden heute in dieser romantischen Kirche wieder Gottesdienste, Konzerte und Hochzeiten statt.

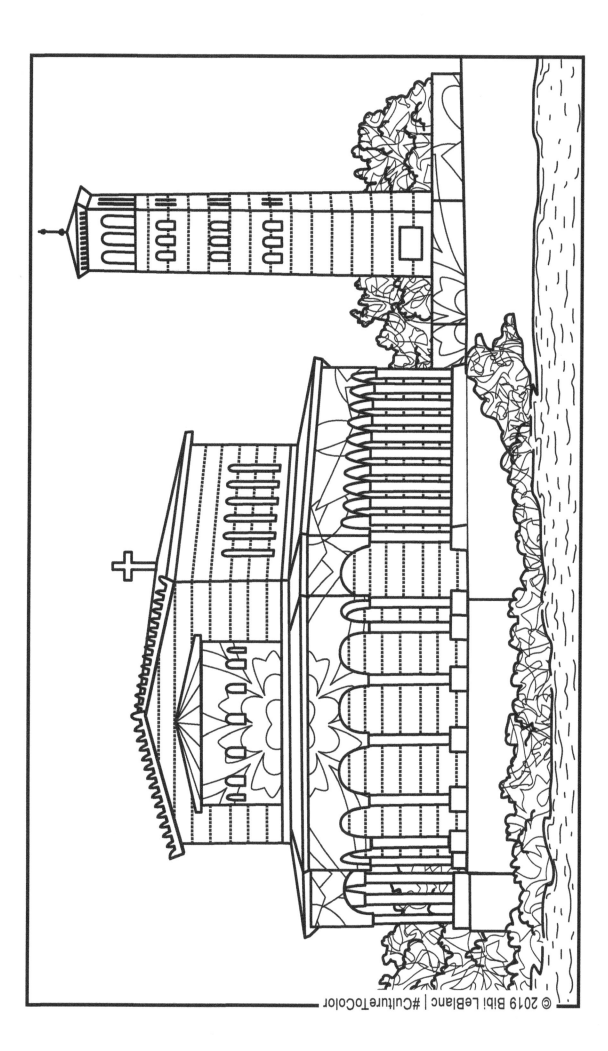

HEILANDSKIRCHE SACROW

## Teufelsberg – Berlin Field Station

*Teufelsberg*, a hill of rubble from World War II, became a Western Allied forces listening station called the *Berlin Field Station*. From the 1950s, antennas and radomes were erected for espionage purposes, intercepting communications and jamming radio signals from the Eastern Bloc. Today, the ruins of the former field station are covered with graffiti and known as the largest and highest street art gallery.

Here, you can still feel the spirit of the Cold War that once permeated the city!

## Teufelsberg

Der *Teufelsberg*, ein Trümmerberg aus dem Zweiten Weltkrieg, wurde zur *Berlin Field Station*, einer Abhörstation der West-Alliierten Streitkräfte. Ab den 50er Jahren wurden Antennen und Radome für Spionagezwecke errichtet, um Kommunikation abzufangen und Funksignale aus dem Ostblock zu stören. Heute sind die Ruinen der ehemaligen Radarstation mit Graffiti bemalt und als größte, höchstgelegene Street Art Galerie bekannt. Sie können hier immer noch den Geist des Kalten Krieges spüren, der einst die Stadt durchdrang.

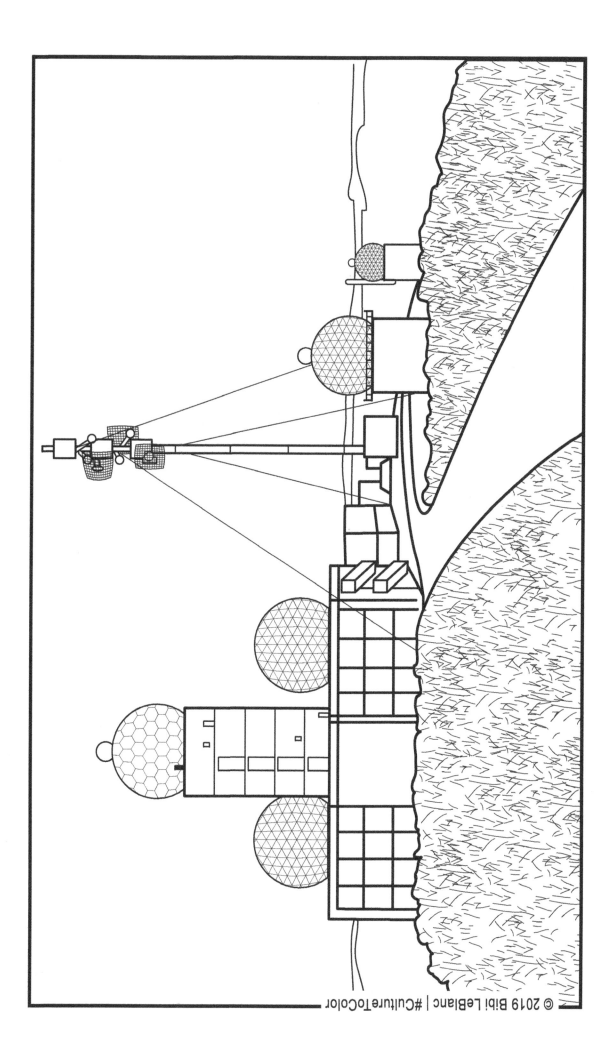

TEUFELSBERG — BERLIN FIELD STATION

## Reichstag

At the end of the Second World War, the *Reichstag* building stood as a partial ruin in the midst of devastation. The starving population used the open spaces surrounding the building to grow potatoes and vegetables. During the division of Berlin, the Reichstag was in the British sector, in the immediate vicinity of the Berlin Wall. The shattered Reichstag became a symbol — a "sandstone colossus in no man's land between the hostile world systems." In 1955, the Bundestag decided to restore the building. On October 4, 1990, the first session of the German Bundestag took place in reunified Germany in the Reichstag building.

## Reichstag

Am Ende des Zweiten Weltkrieges stand das *Reichstagsgebäude* als Teilruine in einer von Trümmern geprägten Umgebung. Die Freiflächen ringsherum dienten der hungernden Bevölkerung für den Anbau von Kartoffeln und Gemüse. Während der Teilung Berlins lag das Reichstagsgebäude im Britischen Sektor in unmittelbarer Nähe der Berliner Mauer. Der zerschossene Reichstag wurde zum Symbol als „Sandsteinkoloß im Niemandsland zwischen den feindlichen Weltsystemen". 1955 beschloss der Bundestag die völlige Wiederherstellung. Am 4. Oktober 1990 fand die erste Sitzung des Deutschen Bundestages im wiedervereinten Deutschland im Reichstagsgebäude statt.

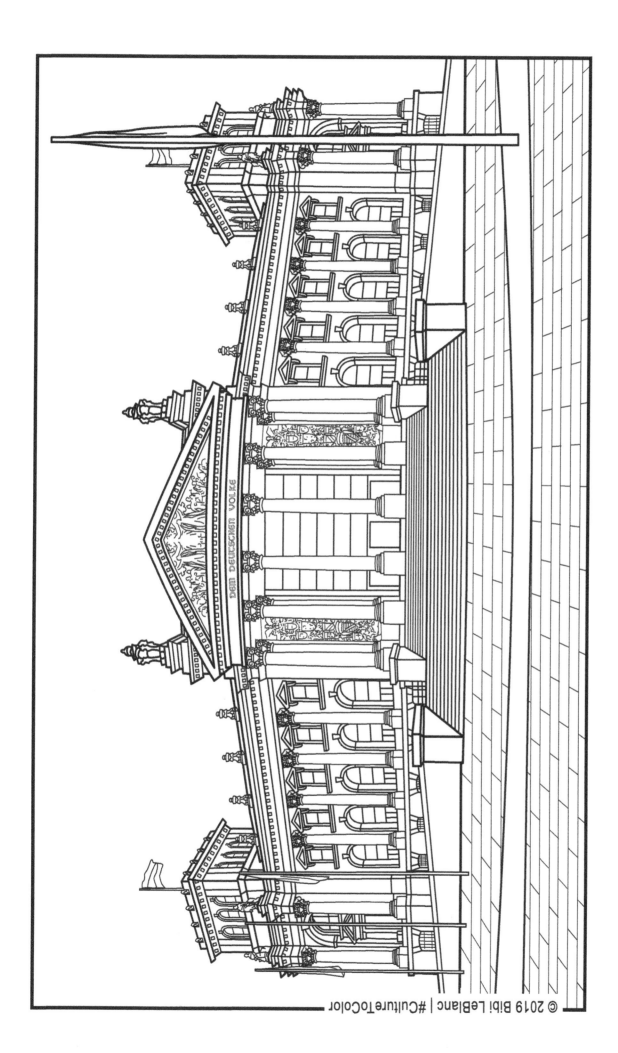

REICHSTAG

## Glienicke Bridge - Bridge of Spies

*Glienicke Bridge* spans the River Havel connecting Berlin with Potsdam. During the Cold War, the bridge was closed to civilians. Of all the checkpoints, the Glienicke Bridge was the only one under Soviet control. It is known as *Bridge of Spies* because it served as the site where captured Warsaw Pact agents would be exchanged for unmasked Western spies. Steven Spielberg's *Bridge of Spies*, the story of the 1962 exchange of agent Francis Gary Powers (USA) for Rudolf Abel (USSR), was filmed here in 2015.

## Glienicker Brücke

Die *Glienicker Brücke* führt über die Havel und verbindet Berlin mit Potsdam. Während des Kalten Krieges war die Brücke für Zivilisten gesperrt. Von allen Kontrollpunkten war die Glienicker Brücke der einzige, der unter sowjetischer Kontrolle stand. Sie ist auch als „Agentenbrücke" bekannt, da hier mehrfach gefangene Agenten des Warschauer Paktes gegen enttarnte westliche Spione ausgetauscht wurden. In Steven Spielbergs Film *Bridge of Spies* (2015) wurde die Geschichte des Austauschs von Agent Francis Gary Powers (USA) gegen Rudolf Abel (UdSSR) im Jahr 1962 hier am Originalschauplatz gedreht.

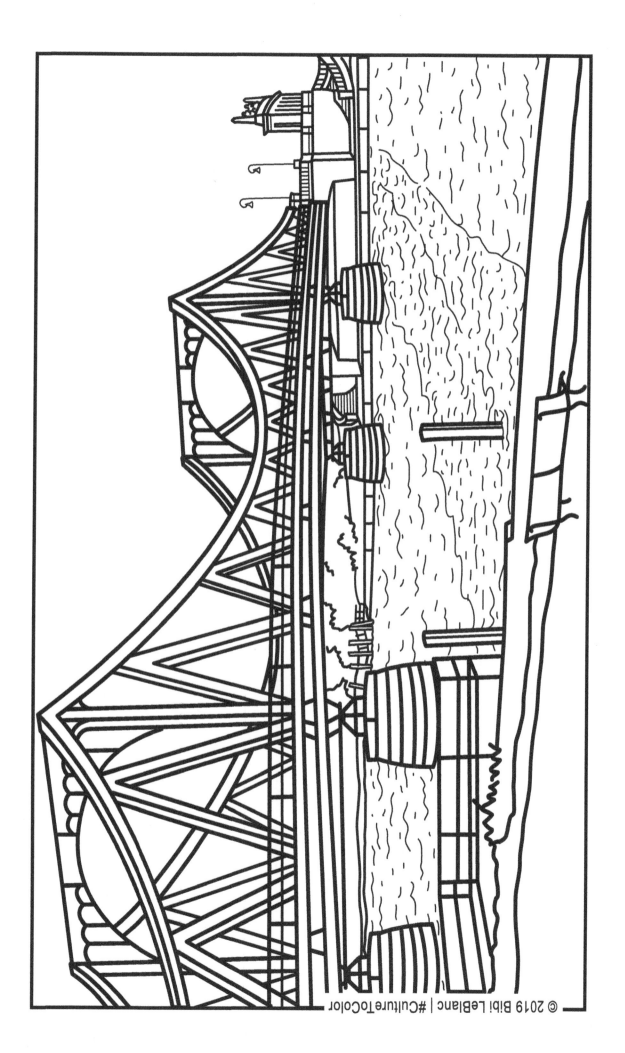

GLIENICKER BRÜCKE — BRIDGE OF SPIES

# Willy Brandt

*Willy Brandt* (1913 – 1992) served as Governing Mayor of Berlin during a period of increasing tension in East-West relations from 1957 to 1966. Brandt was an outspoken critic of Soviet repression. He was the leader of the Social Democratic Party of Germany from 1964 to 1987 and served as Chancellor of the Federal Republic of Germany from 1969 to 1974. As Chancellor, he maintained West Germany's close ties with the United States. For his *Ostpolitik*, which contributed much to the improvement of relations with Eastern Europe, Willy Brandt received the Nobel Peace Prize in 1971.

# Willy Brandt

In einer Zeit zunehmender Spannungen in den Ost-West-Beziehungen war *Willy Brandt* (1913 - 1992) von 1957 bis 1966 Regierender Bürgermeister von West-Berlin. Brandt war ein ausgesprochener Kritiker der sowjetischen Unterdrückung. Von 1964 bis 1987 war er Vorsitzender der SPD und von 1969 bis 1974 Kanzler der Bundesrepublik Deutschland. Als Bundeskanzler hielt er die enge Verbindung Westdeutschlands mit den Vereinigten Staaten aufrecht. Für seine Ostpolitik, die viel zur Verbesserung der Beziehungen zu Osteuropa beitrug, erhielt Willy Brandt 1971 den Friedensnobelpreis.

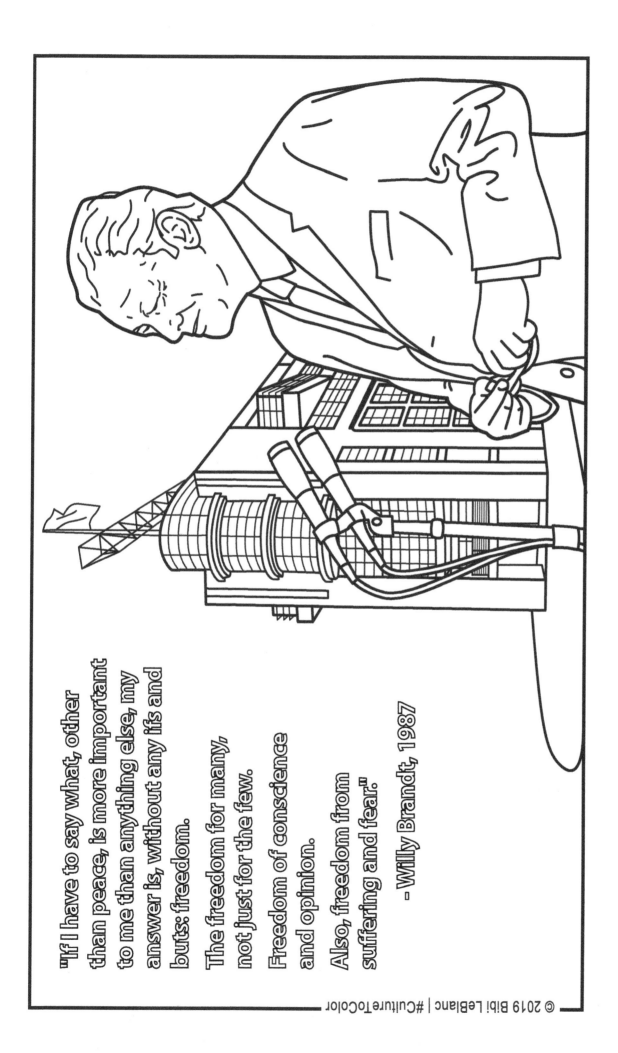

"If I have to say what, other than peace, is more important to me than anything else, my answer is, without any ifs and buts: freedom.

The freedom for many, not just for the few.

Freedom of conscience and opinion.

Also, freedom from suffering and fear."

- Willy Brandt, 1987

WILLY BRANDT

## Haus der Kulturen der Welt - House of the Cultures of the World

The *Haus der Kulturen der Welt* was the USA's contribution to the INTERBAU 1957 building exhibition in Berlin. It became a symbol of the friendship between the United States and West Germany in postwar Berlin. The design was intended to serve as a beacon of freedom. The curved roof bears a striking resemblance to wings and upheld the promise that there would be no restrictions on the freedom of intellectual work. Today, the *House of the Cultures of the World* is an arts venue, exhibition and cultural center and a forum for free expression of opinions.

## Haus der Kulturen der Welt

Das direkt an der Spree erbaute *Haus der Kulturen der Welt* war der Beitrag der USA zur Berliner Bauausstellung INTERBAU 1957. Es wurde zum Symbol für die Freundschaft zwischen den USA und West-Deutschland im Nachkriegs-Berlin. Das Design sollte als Symbol und Leuchtfeuer der Freiheit dienen. Das geschwungene Dach erinnert auffallend an Flügel und versprach, die geistige Arbeitsfreiheit nicht einzuschränken. Heute ist das Haus der Kulturen der Welt Kunst-, Ausstellungs- und Kulturzentrum und Forum für freie Meinungsäußerung.

HAUS DER KULTUREN DER WELT
HOUSE OF THE CULTURES OF THE WORLD

## KaDeWe - Department Store of the West

The *KaDeWe*, short for *Kaufhaus des Westens*, is the best-known department store in Germany and one of the largest in Europe, along with Harrods in London and the Galeries Lafayette in Paris. Since opening in 1907, the store has offered an attractive mix of luxury goods. At the time of the Cold War, KaDeWe became a symbol of the regained economic power of West Germany during the *Wirtschaftswunder* economic boom.

Today, the KaDeWe is an international department store that offers designer goods and exclusive brands and is famous for its legendary delicatessen department.

## KaDeWe

Das *Kaufhaus des Westens*, kurz KaDeWe, ist das bekannteste Kaufhaus in Deutschland, und neben Harrods in London und Galeries Lafayette in Paris, eines der größten in Europa. Seit seiner Eröffnung im Jahr 1907 bietet das Kaufhaus eine attraktive Mischung aus gehobenen- und Luxusgütern. In den Jahren des Kalten Krieges wurde das KaDeWe während des Wirtschaftswunders zum Symbol für die wiedererlangte Wirtschaftskraft West-Deutschlands. Heute ist das KaDeWe ein internationales Kaufhaus, das Designerwaren und exklusive Marken anbietet und berühmt ist für seine legendäre Feinkostabteilung.

KADEWE — DEPARTMENT STORE OF THE WEST

KAUFHAUS DES WESTENS

BERLIN ❤❤ YOU

# Oberbaumbrücke – Oberbaum Bridge & East Side Gallery

The *Oberbaumbrücke*, built 1894 – 1896, spans the Spree River. From 1961 to 1989, it was a border checkpoint and could be used only by pedestrians.

Walk to the nearby *East Side Gallery*, the 4317-foot-long open-air gallery of painted pieces of the Berlin Wall. It is the longest continuous section of the wall  still in existence and is protected as a historical monument. Take photos of the beautiful Oberbaum  Bridge from here, or enjoy a sunset with a view of the city center.

# Oberbaumbrücke & East Side Gallery

Die von 1894 bis 1896 gebaute *Oberbaumbrücke* überspannt die Spree. Von 1961 bis 1989 war sie ein Grenzkontrollpunkt und konnte nur von Fußgängern benutzt werden.

Entdecken Sie von hier  aus die nahe gelegene *East Side Gallery*, die 1316 m lange Freiluftgalerie bemalter Mauerstücke.  Es ist der längste heute noch zusammenhängende Abschnitt der Berliner Mauer und steht unter Denkmalschutz. Machen Sie von hier aus Fotos von der schönen Oberbaumbrücke oder genießen  Sie einen Sonnenuntergang mit Blick auf die Innenstadt.

@OBERBAUMBRÜCKE
@OBERBAUM BRIDGE AND EAST SIDE GALLERY

## Berliner Dom – Berlin Cathedral

*The Berliner Dom (Berlin Cathedral)* with its magnificent dome and golden cross is located on Museum Island in the River Spree. It is a major attraction in Berlin's cityscape. This impressive basilica with its elaborate decorative and ornamental interior contains beautiful mosaics and religious images. It tells fascinating stories of queens and kings in the Hohenzollern family crypt. The history of the church on the island dates back to the 15th century. Daily services as well as more than 100 concerts and other events are held in the Berlin Cathedral every year.

## Berliner Dom

Der *Berliner Dom* mit seiner prächtigen Kuppel und dem goldenen Kreuz befindet sich auf der Museumsinsel in der Spree. Er ist eine der Hauptattraktionen im Berliner Stadtbild. Diese eindrucksvolle Basilika mit ihrem kunstvollen dekorativen und ornamentalen Interieur enthält wunderschöne Mosaiken, religiöse Bilder und erzählt faszinierende Geschichten von Königinnen und Königen in der Hohenzollern-Familiengruft. Die Geschichte der Kirche auf der Insel reicht bis ins 15. Jahrhundert zurück. Im Berliner Dom finden täglich Gottesdienste und jedes Jahr über 100 Konzerte und Veranstaltungen statt.

BERLINER DOM — BERLIN CATHEDRAL

# Trabant

Lovingly called *"Trabi,"* the *Trabant* automobile has become a symbol of former East Germany. The *"spark plug with a roof"* has a plastic body and two-stroke engine. People had to wait 10+ years to get one. The 1980s model had no tachometer, headlights or turn-signal indicators, no fuel gauge or rear seat belts, no external fuel door and used a gasoline/oil mixture. It took 21 seconds to get from 0 to 60 mph, and had a top speed of 70 mph. Trabant means fellow traveler, or satellite. Its name was inspired by the Russian satellite Sputnik, which went into space in 1957, the year the Trabi was first built.

# Trabant

Der liebevoll „Trabi" genannte *Trabant* ist zu einem Symbol der ehemaligen DDR geworden. Die „Zündkerze mit Dach" hat eine Plastikkarosserie und einen Zweitaktmotor. Die Wartezeit für einen Trabi betrug mehr als 10 Jahre. Das Modell der 80er Jahre hatte keinen Drehzahlmesser, keine Scheinwerfer-, Blinker- oder Tankanzeiger, keine hinteren Sicherheitsgurte, keine externe Tankklappe, und verwendete ein Benzin/Öl-Gemisch. Es dauerte 21 Sekunden, um von 0 auf 100 km/h zu kommen, und die Höchstgeschwindigkeit betrug 112 km/h. Der Name Trabant bedeutet „Mitreisender" oder „Satellit", inspiriert vom russischen Satelliten „Sputnik", der 1957 in den Weltraum flog.

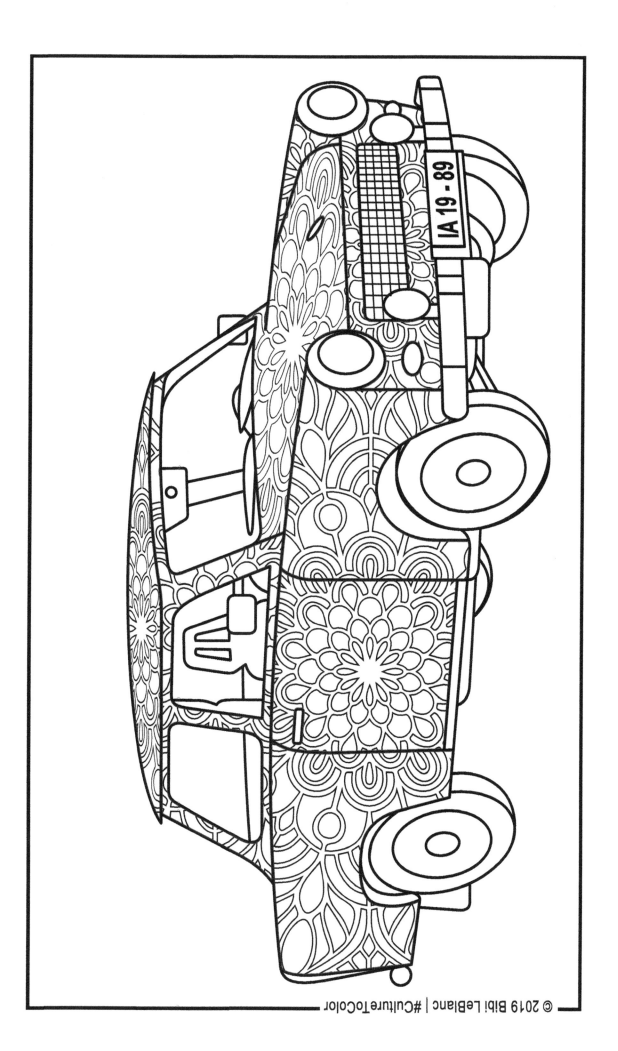

TRABANT

## Philharmonie Berlin

The *Philharmonie* has been the musical heart of Berlin since 1963. Designed by architect Hans Scharoun, its unusual tentlike shape and innovative concert-hall design with vineyard-style seating arrangements, initially ignited controversy but now serves as a model for concert halls around the world. Shortly before the Philharmonie opened in 1963, experts used pistol shots to test the acoustics – and that's how the Philharmonie came to have its perfect sound. Since the fall of the Berlin Wall it has become part of the new urban center Kulturforum at Potsdamer Platz.

## Philharmonie Berlin

Die *Philharmonie* ist seit 1963 das musikalische Herz Berlins. Das vom Architekten Hans Scharoun entworfene ungewöhnliche zeltähnliche Design und die innovative Konzertsaal-Architektur mit Sitzgruppen im Weinbergstil lösten zunächst Kontroversen aus, dienen heute jedoch als Vorbild für Konzertsäle auf der ganzen Welt. Kurz vor der Eröffnung der Philharmonie im Jahr 1963 testeten Experten mit Pistolenschüssen die Akustik – und so kam die Philharmonie zu einem perfekten Klang. Seit dem Fall der Berliner Mauer ist die Philharmonie Teil des neuen Stadtzentrums Kulturforum am Potsdamer Platz geworden.

PHILHARMONIE BERLIN

## Schloss Charlottenburg – Charlottenburg Palace

This beautiful palace was built at the end of the 17th century. Sophie Charlotte, the first Queen consort of Prussia, was an accomplished musician, playing the harpsichord and singing Italian opera. She often strolled through the grounds with her friend, the renowned scholar and philosopher Gottfried Wilhelm Leibniz. When Sophie Charlotte died, just 36 years old, the palace and the area around it were named after her: *Charlottenburg*. Today, *Schloss Charlottenburg* is the largest and most magnificent palace in Berlin – a highlight for any Berlin visitor. — Fun Fact: Napoleon stayed here in 1806.

## Schloss Charlottenburg

Dieser wunderschöne Palast wurde Ende des 17. Jahrhunderts erbaut. Sophie Charlotte, die erste Königin von Preußen, war eine versierte Musikerin, die Cembalo spielte und italienische Opern sang. Oft schlenderte sie mit ihrem Freund, dem bekannten Gelehrten und Philosophen Gottfried Wilhelm Leibniz, durch das Gelände. Nach dem Tod der 36-jährigen Sophie Charlotte wurden das *Schloss* und die Umgebung nach ihr benannt: *Charlottenburg*. Heute ist es das größte und prächtigste Schloss Berlins - ein Highlight für jeden Berlin-Besucher. — Fun Fact: *Napoleon übernachtete 1806 hier.*

SCHLOSS CHARLOTTENBURG

# Tränenpalast – Palace of Tears

Tears and longing, anger and despair, hope and fear — at hardly any other location was the emotional experience of crossing the border as intense as at the *Tränenpalast*. It is a former border crossing point between East and West Berlin at Friedrichstraße station. Here, in an atmosphere of harassment and intimidation, people experienced firsthand the powerful impact of the division of Germany: waiting times of several hours, harsh tones and severe gazes from the *Vopos* (border guards) and the fear of permission being denied arbitrarily. Today the Tränenpalast is home of the permanent exhibit

"Border Experiences - Site of German Division".

# Tränenpalast

Tränen und Sehnsucht, Wut und Verzweiflung, Hoffnung und Angst - an kaum einem anderen Ort war das emotionale Erlebnis, die Grenze zu überqueren, so intensiv wie am *Tränenpalast*. An diesem ehemaligen Grenzübergang zwischen Ost- und West-Berlin am Bahnhof Friedrichstraße haben die Menschen die Auswirkungen der Teilung Deutschlands hautnah erlebt. Es herrschte eine Atmosphäre der Belästigung und Einschüchterung: Wartezeiten von mehreren Stunden, harsche Töne und strenge Blicke der Vopos und die Angst, dass die Erlaubnis willkürlich verweigert wird. Heute befindet sich im Tränenpalast die ständige Ausstellung "Grenzerfahrungen - Alltag der deutschen Teilung".

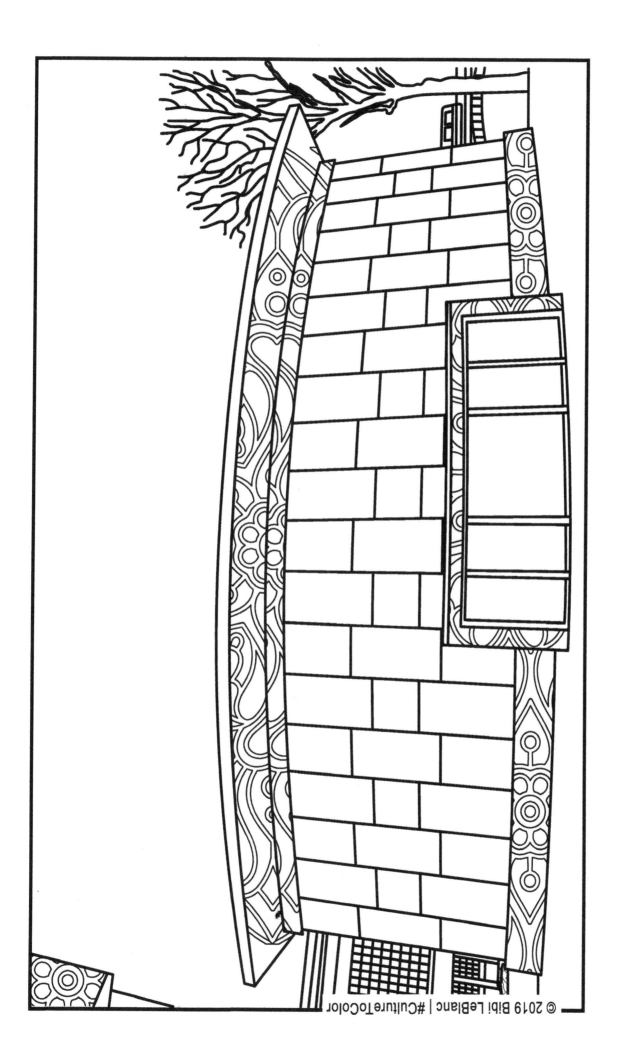

TRÄNENPALAST — PALACE OF TEARS

## Rotes Rathaus und Neptunbrunnen – Red City Hall & Neptune Fountain

The *Rotes Rathaus (Red City Hall)*, then located in the Soviet sector, served as the town hall of East Berlin. After reunification, the administration of Berlin officially moved into the Rotes Rathaus.

The *Neptune Fountain*, built in 1891, depicts the Roman god Neptune in the center. The four women around him represent the main rivers of Prussia at the time the fountain was constructed: the Elbe (fruits and ears of corn), Rhine (fishnet and grapes), Vistula (wooden blocks, symbols of forestry), and Oder (goats and animal skins).

## Rotes Rathaus & Neptunbrunnen

Das *Rote Rathaus* diente während der Teilung als Rathaus von Ost-Berlin. Nach der Wiedervereinigung zog die Verwaltung Berlins offiziell in das Rote Rathaus ein.

Der 1891 erbaute *Neptunbrunnen* zeigt im Zentrum den römischen Gott Neptun. Die vier Frauen um ihn herum repräsentieren die wichtigsten Flüsse Preußens zum Zeitpunkt des Brunnenbaus: Elbe (Früchte und Ähren), Rhein (Fischnetz und Trauben), Weichsel (Holzblöcke, Symbole der Forstwirtschaft) und Oder (Ziegen und Tierhäute).

ROTES RATHAUS UND NEPTUNBRUNNEN —
RED CITY HALL AND NEPTUNE FOUNTAIN

## Ronald Reagan - Address at the Brandenburg Gate, June 12, 1987

*"Behind me stands a wall that encircles the free sectors of this city, part of a vast system of barriers that divides the entire continent of Europe. Standing before the Brandenburg Gate, every man is a German separated from his fellow men. ... As long as this gate is closed, ...it is the question of freedom for all mankind."*

*President Reagan continued, "General Secretary Gorbachev, if you seek peace, if you seek prosperity for the Soviet Union and Eastern Europe, if you seek liberalization: Come here to this gate. Mr. Gorbachev, open this gate.*

*Mr. Gorbachev -- Mr. Gorbachev, tear down this wall!"*

## Ronald Reagan – Ansprache am Brandenburger Tor, 12. Juni 1987

*„Hinter mir befindet sich eine Mauer, die die freien Bereiche dieser Stadt umgibt und Teil eines riesigen Barrieresystems ist, das den gesamten europäischen Kontinent teilt. Jeder vor dem Brandenburger Tor stehende Mensch ist ein von seinen Mitmenschen getrennter Deutscher. Solange dieses Tor geschlossen ist, bleibt nicht nur die deutsche Frage offen, sondern die Frage der Freiheit für die ganze Menschheit.*

*„Generalsekretär Gorbatschow, wenn Sie Frieden suchen, wenn Sie Wohlstand für die Sowjetunion und Osteuropa suchen, wenn Sie Liberalisierung anstreben, kommen Sie hierher zu diesem Tor.*

*Herr Gorbatschow, öffnen Sie dieses Tor!*

*Herr Gorbatschow -- Herr Gorbatschow, reißen Sie diese Mauer nieder!"‟*

"Tear down this wall"

RONALD REAGAN—ADDRESS AT THE
BRANDENBURG GATE, JUNE 12, 1987

# Gendarmenmarkt

The *Gendarmenmarkt* is said to be the most beautiful square in Berlin, maybe even in Europe. Relax in one of the cafés and soak in the magnificent view of this unrivaled trio of buildings: the French Cathedral, the Concert Hall and the German Cathedral. Largely destroyed during World War II, it was restored in the 1980s. Thanks to the East-West Cultural Agreement, the Schiller Monument (with its statue of philosopher, poet and historian Friedrich Schiller), in storage in West Berlin, was returned to its rightful home outside the Konzerthaus in the Gendarmenmarkt square in East Berlin.

# Gendarmenmarkt

Er ist einer der schönsten Plätze in Berlin, vielleicht sogar in Europa: der *Gendarmenmarkt*. Entspannen Sie sich in einem der Cafés und genießen Sie den herrlichen Blick auf dieses einzigartige Gebäude-Trio: Französischer Dom, Konzerthaus und Deutscher Dom. Während des Zweiten Weltkrieges weitgehend zerstört, wurde er in den 80er Jahren restauriert. Dank des Ost-West-Kulturabkommens wurde die in West-Berlin gelagerte Schiller-Statue in ihr rechtmäßiges Zuhause vor dem Konzerthaus in Ost-Berlin, mitten auf dem Gendarmenmarkt, zurückgebracht.

GENDARMENMARKT

## Bundeskanzleramt - German Chancellery

In 1991, two years after the Berlin Wall fell, the Bundestag voted for Berlin to be the capital of a reunited Germany. The *German Chancellery* is set close to the Reichstag parliament building in Berlin. It was designed to embody a clear message of transparency. This modern and elegant complex is part of the *Band des Bundes*, a series of federal buildings spanning the River Spree, linking the eastern and western parts of the long-divided city.

## Bundeskanzleramt

1991, zwei Jahre nach dem Mauerfall, wählte der Bundestag Berlin zur Hauptstadt des wiedervereinigten Deutschlands. Das *Bundeskanzleramt* befindet sich in der Nähe des Reichstagsgebäudes. Es sollte eine klare Botschaft der Transparenz verkörpern. Dieser moderne und elegante Komplex ist Teil des „Band des Bundes", einer Reihe von Bundesgebäuden, die sich über die Spree erstrecken und den Osten und Westen der lange geteilten Stadt verbinden.

BUNDESKANZLERAMT — GERMAN CHANCELLERY

# Berliner Currywurst - Konnopke's Imbiß

The *Currywurst* is the city's most popular fast food, a hot sliced pork sausage covered in curry sauce and curry powder, usually eaten with a small disposable fork from a paper plate. You can find Currywurst stalls throughout the city or go straight to *Konnopke's Imbiß*. Konnopke's has been family-run in Prenzlauer Berg in the former eastern part of Berlin since 1930. *Konnopke's* is located just below the train tracks, and its Currywurst is known well beyond the borders of Berlin.

# Konnopke's Imbiß und die Berliner Currywurst

Die *Currywurst* ist das beliebteste Fast Food der Stadt. Die heiße, in Scheiben geschnittene Wurst mit Currysauce und Currypulver wird meistens mit einer kleinen Einweggabel von einem Pappteller gegessen. Sie finden Currywurstbuden in der ganzen Stadt, oder Sie gehen gleich zu *Konnopke's*. Es ist ein seit 1930 familiengeführter Imbiß in Prenzlauer Berg im ehemaligen Ostteil Berlins. Konnopke's liegt direkt unter den Hochbahngleisen, und seine Currywurst ist weit über die Grenzen Berlins hinaus bekannt.

BERLINER CURRYWURST – KONNOPKE'S IMBIß

# Sony Center – Potsdamer Platz

From 1961 to 1989, most of this area was part of the no man's land of the Berlin Wall. Since the fall of the wall, it has become a part of new cultural center, Kulturforum. The roof construction of the *Sony Center at Potsdamer Platz* is an extraordinary technical achievement. A fanned canvas canopy (with a self-cleaning, Teflon-coated fabric) with its changing light spectacle symbolizes Mount Fuji in Japan. According to the Japanese, the Kami (Shinto gods) live in the mountains. Since Berlin has no mountain, the Sony Center was built as an artificial residence for the Kami, so that Sony is also protected in Europe.

# Sony Center am Potsdamer Platz

Von 1961 bis 1989 gehörte der größte Teil dieser Fläche zum Niemandsland der Berliner Mauer. Seit dem Fall der Mauer ist hier ein neues kulturelles Zentrum entstanden. Die Dachkonstruktion des *Sony Centers am Potsdamer Platz* ist eine aussergewöhnliche technische Leistung. Ein aufgefächertes Zeltdach aus Segeltuch (selbstreinigendes, teflonbeschichtetes Gewebe) mit seinem wechselnden Lichtspektakel symbolisiert Mount Fuji in Japan. Nach japanischer Auffassung leben die Kami (Shinto-Götter) in den Bergen. Da Berlin aber keinen Berg hat, wurde das Sony Center als künstliche Residenz für die Kami errichtet, damit Sony auch in Europa geschützt ist.

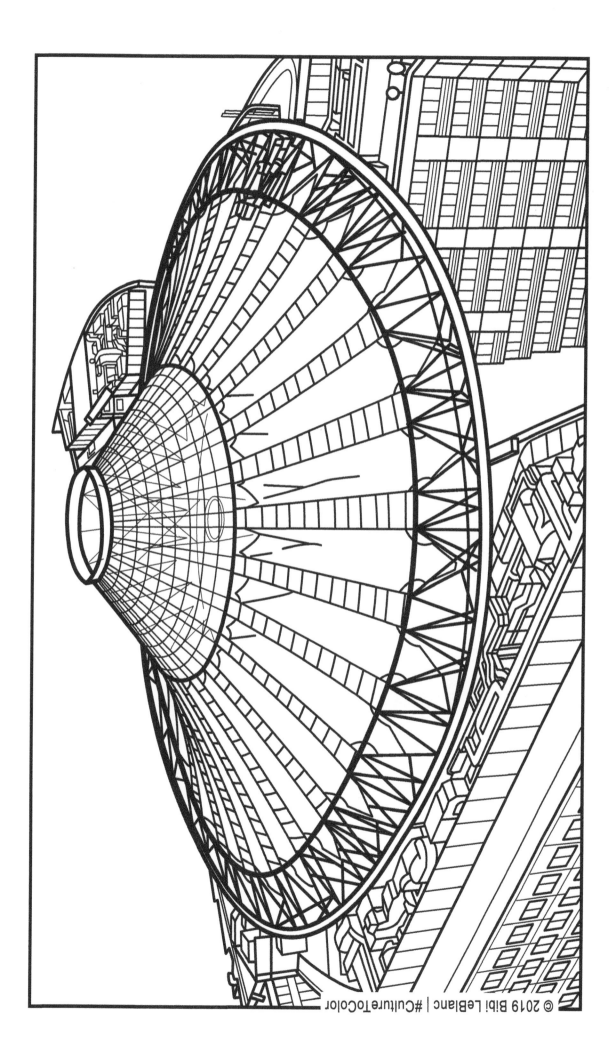

SONY CENTER — POTSDAMER PLATZ

# Museum Island

Situated in the heart of Berlin in the River Spree, *Museum Island* with its unparalleled ensemble of museums, showcases magnificent collections of art and cultural artifacts. Home to the legendary bust of Nefertiti, the Pergamon Altar and the stunning Ishtar Gate, the Museum Island complex was designated a UNESCO World Heritage Site in 1999. Following the reunification of Germany, the collections of former East and West Berlin were merged. Museum Island is home to the Pergamon Museum, Bode Museum, Neues Museum (New Museum), Alte Nationalgalerie (Old National Gallery), Altes Museum (Old Museum), as well as the new James-Simon-Galerie.

# Museumsinsel

Die im Herzen Berlins an der Spree gelegene *Museumsinsel* mit ihrem herausragenden Museumsensemble zeigt großartige Kunst- und Kultursammlungen. Die Museumsinsel mit der legendären Büste der Nofretete, dem Pergamonaltar und dem beeindruckenden Ischtar-Tor wurde 1999 zum UNESCO-Weltkulturerbe erklärt. Nach der Wiedervereinigung Deutschlands wurden die Sammlungen des ehemaligen Ost- und West-Berlins zusammengelegt. Auf der Museumsinsel befinden sich: Pergamonmuseum, Bode-Museum, Neues Museum, Alte Nationalgalerie, Altes Museum und die neue James-Simon-Galerie.

MUSEUMSINSEL — MUSEUM ISLAND

# Fall of the Berlin Wall

On November 9, 1989, after months of peaceful protests in East Germany, the unimaginable happened: A spokesman for East Berlin's Communist Party made a fateful mistake by announcing travel restrictions would be eased *immediately*. East and West Berliners flocked to the wall, chanting "Tor auf!" ("Open the gate!"). Under pressure from the masses, without instructions from their superiors and to avoid violence, the border commanders decided to open the gates on their own authority. More than 2 million people from East Berlin visited West Berlin that weekend to participate in a celebration that was, as one journalist wrote,

"the greatest street party in the history of the world."

"Only today," one Berliner spray-painted on a piece of the wall, "is the war really over."

# Mauerfall

Am 9. November 1989, nach Monaten friedlicher Proteste in Ostdeutschland, ereignete sich das Unvorstellbare: Ein Sprecher der Kommunistischen Partei Ostberlins machte einen schicksalshaften Fehler als er das *sofortige* Aufheben der Reisebeschränkungen verkündete. Ost- und West-Berliner strömten zur Mauer und sangen „Tor auf! Tor auf!" Unter dem Druck der Massen, fehlenden Anweisungen der Vorgesetzten und um Gewalt zu vehindern, beschlossen Grenzkommandanten schließlich eigenmächtig, die Grenzübergänge zu öffnen. Mehr als 2 Millionen Menschen aus Ost-Berlin besuchten West- Berlin an diesem Wochenende, um an einer Feier teilzunehmen, die, wie ein Journalist schrieb,

„die größte Straßenparty in der Geschichte der Welt" war.

„Erst heute", sprühte ein Berliner auf die Mauer, „ist der Krieg wirklich vorbei".

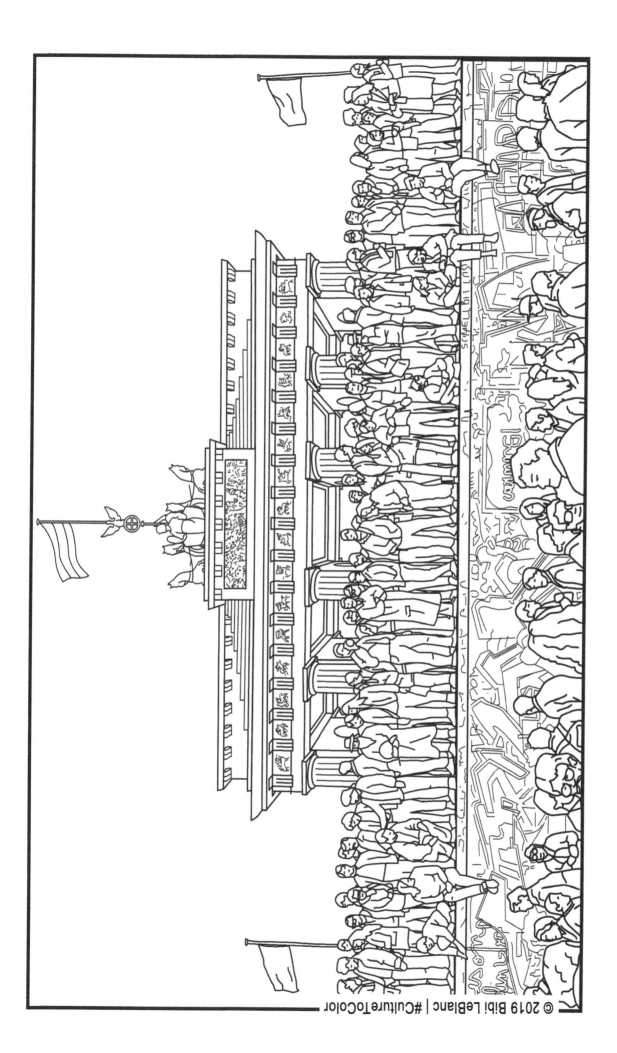

MAUERFALL — FALL OF THE BERLIN WALL

## Brandenburg Gate

Until the beginning of the construction of the Berlin Wall in 1961, everyone could travel freely through Berlin's iconic *Brandenburg Gate*. After the wall was built, the Brandenburg Gate was isolated and remained a focus of the world's attention as it symbolized Berlin's Cold War division into East and West. On December 22, 1989, the official re-opening of the Brandenburg Gate took place to the cheers of more than 100,000 people. The opening of the Brandenburg Gate foreshadowed the reunification of East and West Germany.

## Brandenburger Tor

Bis zum Beginn des Baus der Berliner Mauer am 13. August 1961 konnte sich jeder frei durch Berlins Wahrzeichen, das *Brandenburger Tor*, bewegen. Nach dem Mauerbau war das Brandenburger Tor zwar 28 Jahre lang isoliert, stand aber als Symbol für die Teilung Berlins noch immer im Fokus der Weltöffentlichkeit. Am 22. Dezember 1989 fand unter dem Jubel von mehr als 100.000 Menschen die offizielle Wiedereröffnung des Brandenburger Tors statt. Die Öffnung des Brandenburger Tors war ein Vorbote der Wiedervereinigung beider deutscher Länder.

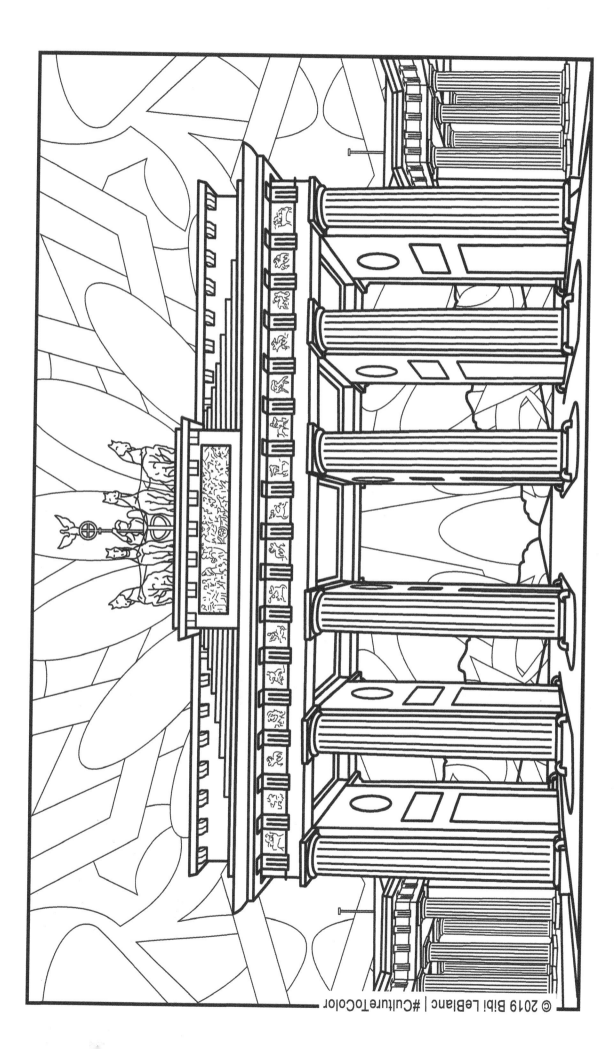

BRANDENBURGER TOR — BRANDENBURG GATE

## Skyline

Berlin's history has left the city with an eclectic assortment of architecture. The city's appearance in the 21st century has been shaped by the key role the city played in Germany's 20th-century history. Each of the governments based in Berlin added its distinct flavor to the city's architecture and *skyline* through ambitious construction programs.

## Skyline

Berlins Geschichte hat die Stadt mit einem vielseitigen Angebot an Architektur hinterlassen. Das Erscheinungsbild der Stadt im 21. Jahrhundert wurde von der Schlüsselrolle der Stadt in der deutschen Geschichte des 20. Jahrhunderts geprägt. Jede der in Berlin ansässigen Regierungen initiierte ehrgeizige Bauprogramme, die der Architektur und der *Skyline* der Stadt ihren eigenen Charakter verliehen.

Culture to Color

Berlin Divided – Berlin United

SKYLINE

## A Blank Canvas

What did you like best and enjoy most? What inspired you during your visit to Berlin? Here's your chance to get creative. I would love to see your creation. You can send it to me at Bibi@CultureToColor.com.

## Eine unbemalte Leinwand

Was hat Ihnen in Berlin am Besten gefallen? Was hat Sie fasziniert oder inspiriert? Hier können Sie kreativ sein und Ihr eigenes Bild entwerfen. Sie können es mir gerne schicken: Bibi@CultureToColor.com

UNBEMALTE LEINWAND – BLANK CANVAS

## Buddy Bear

The bear has long been the symbol on Berlin's coat of arms. Klaus and Eva Herlitz, along with sculptor Roman Strobl, developed the *Buddy Bear* project in 2001. You can find about 350 hand-painted Buddy Bears located throughout Berlin. The original Buddy Bears are posed standing with both arms up in the air as a symbol of kindliness and optimism. The now traveling *United Buddy Bears* exhibition promotes tolerance and peace among the world's many different religions and cultural groups.

## Buddy Bär

Der Bär ist seit langem das Wahrzeichen des Berliner Wappens. Klaus und Eva Herlitz entwickelten 2001, zusammen mit dem Bildhauer Roman Strobl, das *Buddy Bär*-Projekt. Sie finden ungefähr 350 handbemalte Buddy Bären in ganz Berlin. Die originalen Buddy Bären stehen mit beiden Armen in der Luft als Symbol für Freundlichkeit und  Optimismus. Die jetzt reisende Ausstellung der *United Buddy Bears* fördert Toleranz  und Frieden unter den vielen verschiedenen Religionen und kulturellen Gruppen der Welt.

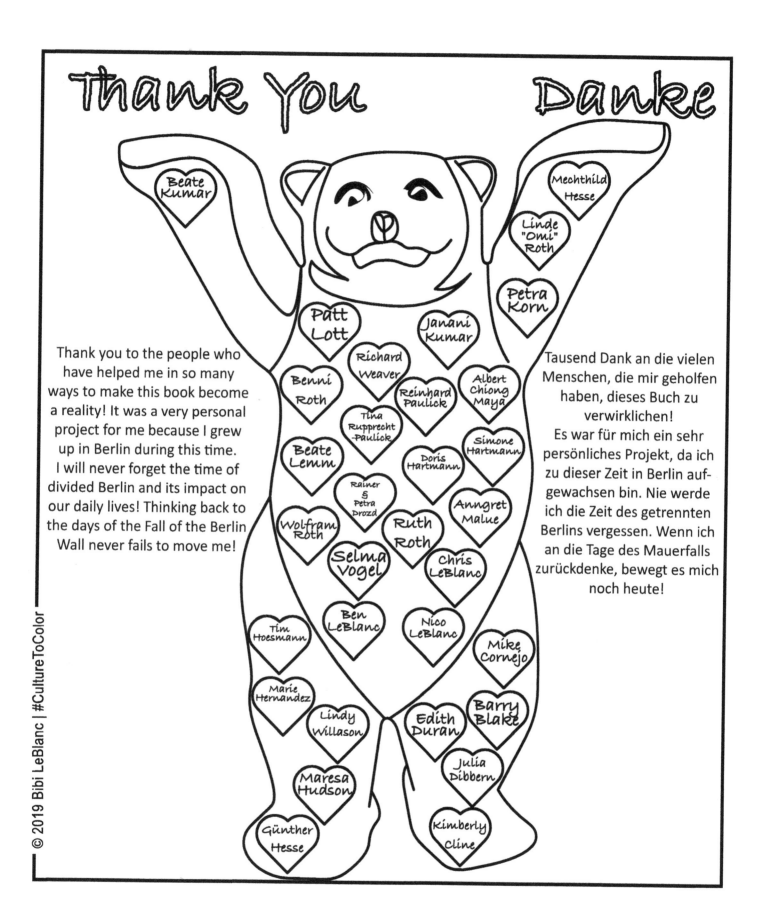

Thank You    Danke

Thank you to the people who have helped me in so many ways to make this book become a reality! It was a very personal project for me because I grew up in Berlin during this time. I will never forget the time of divided Berlin and its impact on our daily lives! Thinking back to the days of the Fall of the Berlin Wall never fails to move me!

Tausend Dank an die vielen Menschen, die mir geholfen haben, dieses Buch zu verwirklichen! Es war für mich ein sehr persönliches Projekt, da ich zu dieser Zeit in Berlin aufgewachsen bin. Nie werde ich die Zeit des getrennten Berlins vergessen. Wenn ich an die Tage des Mauerfalls zurückdenke, bewegt es mich noch heute!

BUDDY BÄR

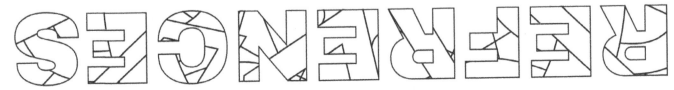

# REFERENCES

## Websites & Sources

A special Thank you to these websites and institutions for providing detailed information about the sights in this book.

- **Berlin.de**
- **History.com**
- **Visitberlin.de**
- **Washingtonpost.com**
- **Wikipedia.org**
- **Berliner Dom** - berlinerdom.de/en
- **Buddy Bär** - buddy-baer.com
- **Bundeskanzleramt** - bundesregierung.de/breg-en/
- **Culture to Color** – culturetocolor.com
- **East Side Gallery** - eastsidegalleryberlin.de/en/
- **Fernsehturm** - tv-turm.de/en
- **Flughafen Tempelhof** - thf-berlin.de/en/
- **Funkturm Berlin** - funkturm-messeberlin.de/
- **GDR Watchtower** - berlinwallexpo.de/en/
- **Gendarmenmarkt** - gendarmenmarkt.de/home-english.htm
- **Haus der Kulturen** - hkw.de/en
- **Heilandskirche** - heilandskirche-sacrow.de
- **Hotel Adlon Kempinski** - kempinski.com/en/berlin/hotel-adlon
- **KaDeWe** - kadewe.de/en
- **Kaiser Wilhelm Gedächtniskirche** - gedaechtniskirche-berlin.de
- **Konnopke's Imbiss** - konnopke-imbiss.de/en
- **Luftbrücke – Airlift** - alliiertenmuseum.de/themen/berliner-luftbruecke
- **Museumsinsel:**
- **Altes Museum (Old Museum)** - smb.museum/en/museums-institutions/altes-museum
- **Alte Nationalgalerie (Old National Gallery)** - smb.museum/museum/museen-und-einrichtungen/alte-nationalgalerie
- **Bode Museum** - smb.museum/en/museums-institutions/bode-museum
- **James Simon Gallery** - smb.museum/en/museums-institutions/james-simon-galerie
- **Neues Museum (New Museum)** - smb.museum/en/museums-institutions/neues-museum
- **Pergamon Museum** - smb.museum/en/museums-institutions/pergamonmuseum
- **Reichstag** - bundestag.de/en/
- **Philharmonie** - berliner-philharmoniker.de/en/
- **Potsdamer Platz** - potsdamerplatz.de/en
- **Schloss Charlottenburg** - spsg.de/schloesser-gaerten/objekt/schloss-charlottenburg-altes-schloss/
- **Sony Center** - sonycenter.de/en
- **Staatsoper** - staatsoper-berlin.de/en
- **Teufelsberg** - teufelsberg-berlin.de
- **Tierpark Berlin** - tierpark-berlin.de/en
- **Timeline** - oxfordreference.com/view/10.1093/acref/9780191737909.timeline.0001
- **Tränenpalast** - hdg.de/en/
- **Wall Museum – Haus am Checkpoint Charlie** - mauermuseum.de/en
- **Weltzeituhr** - weltzeituhr-berlin.de
- **Willy Brandt Stiftung** - willy-brandt.de/en/the-foundation/
- **Zoologischer Garten** - zoo-berlin.de/en

CULTURE TO COLOR

For the artist in you - coloring adventures around the globe.
Für den Künstler in Ihnen - Ausmal-Abenteuer rund um die Welt.